# Bar Fishing
## the
# Lower Fraser River

Hugh Heighton

ISBN 0-88839-237-0
Copyright © 1989 Hugh Heighton

Second printing 1994

**Cataloging in Publication Data**
Heighton, Hugh, 1940-
    Bar fishing the lower Fraser River


    ISBN 0-88839-237-0

    1. Fishing—British Columbia—Fraser River.
I. Title.
SH572.B7H44 1989   799.1'1'0971133   C89-091434-6

Printed in Hong Kong

Edited: Phil Atkinson
Designed: Phil Atkinson

Published simultaneously in Canada and the United States by

**HANCOCK HOUSE PUBLISHERS LTD.**
**19313 Zero Avenue, Surrey, B.C. V4P 1M7**
**(604) 538-1114    Fax (604) 538-2262**

**HANCOCK HOUSE PUBLISHERS**
**1431 Harrison Avenue, Box 959, Blaine, WA 98231-0959**
**(206) 354-6953    Fax (604) 538-2262**

# Contents

*To*
*Satu,*
*for her patience;*
*and*
*Pat,*
*my fishing buddy and good friend.*

# Introduction

Bar fishing is enjoyed almost year-round in British Columbia. The gear is relatively simple and the technique can be learned by anyone. The term "Bar Fishing" means "still" fishing from a shoreline which is the result of a build up of sand or gravel caused by the action in the river or stream. Some appear only when the water is low enough to make them accessible.

Bar fishing has many advantages over other methods of angling. For example, you can sit in your chair and read your favorite fishing magazine or book. You can scour the sand for lost gear left by others, or get a suntan while preparing a tasty meal over an open campfire. And while all this is going on, you're still fishing. (Serious fishermen, however, stand right by their rods ready to set the hook at the very slightest movement of the rod tip!)

Whatever style of fishing fits your particular personality, the abundant bars along our rivers and streams can offer hours of relaxation with the opportunity of taking home some beautiful, fresh fish.

The Lower Fraser River affords the experienced fisherman, and the neophyte too, many accessible sites for angling; in many cases, literally a line toss from your vehicle.

These bars, as the locals call them, are available from the mouth of the river to Hope and beyond. While there is some truth to the rumor that the small commercial fishing boats take a lion's share of the catch, many sports anglers, myself included, have caught fish up and down the river throughout the year.

The variety of fish in the Fraser ranges from salmon to suckers, and includes coarse fish such as chub, bullhead, and sturgeon, and rainbow trout, cutthroat, Dolly Varden and, of course, the indomitable steelhead.

This book will provide information on some of the most popular sites, how best to reach them, what fish are caught, and tips on the most useful gear and bait to use. Younger anglers can fun-fish many of these bars where they may catch all Fraser species of coarse fish.

> **Note:** *Fishing on the Fraser is subject to Fisheries and Wildlife regulations. Be sure that you have a proper license, depending on where you fish.*

### Assembling the Bar Rig T-Bar

Bar fishing tackle is similar to equipment used in other forms of angling except for its assembly and application. It is basically "still" fishing and the rig setup requires the bait to remain stationary and tangle-free. This is achieved by the use of a bar rig.

Experienced fishermen assemble their own rigs; however, they can be bought already made up in most sporting goods stores.

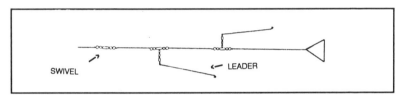

T-bars come in different sizes. They are made from metal and their main purpose is to hold the leader line and bait away from the main line and the weight, preventing tangling.

There are several methods to attach T-bars to the leader line. Some use plastic beads while others jam a toothpick between the line and the T-bar. The toothpick allows the T-bar and the leader to slide down to the weight when a bigger fish is hooked.

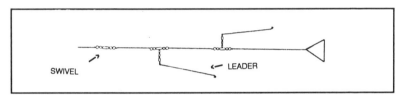

### Hooks

There are many types of fishing hooks on the market. Some are stainless steel, bronze, nickel, etc. Some are machine-sharpened and others are laser-sharpened. (Usually the package will specify laser-sharpened hooks.)

The laser-sharpened hooks are the ones most experienced fishermen use today as they hold their point longer, and, as any fisherman knows, "sharp hooks catch more fish."

### Baiting the Hook for Bar Fishing

Sounds simple, and it is, but you have to know how. The most common baits used in local waters (excluding the ocean) are dew worms, single salmon eggs, and roe. Dew worms and single eggs are fairly easy to apply; simply impale them on the hook. The two methods most fishermen use for baiting the hook with roe are:
1. by placing a small piece of cured roe in the loop of a snelled hook;
2. by placing pieces of roe in small bags of cheesecloth, or other material, and putting the hook through the small bag.

The method depends on current and location.

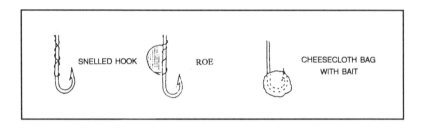

### Cured Roe

Roe usually comes in skeins or chopped up in convenient sizes ready for use. Skeins are the eggs with the membrane still attached and require cutting before use.

Fresh roe is prized by the experienced fisherman and many will go to great lengths and expense to acquire it. Dog roe (chum salmon) is the most sought after, while spring (chinook) and coho roe are easier to aquire at the beginning of the salmon season.

There are many ways to cure roe. The simplest and most commonly used method is to spread the skeins of roe on soft paper overnight, allowing the roe to drain and become firm enough for use. Then sprinkle the skeins with Borax and they are ready to be used. Some substitute coarse salt for the Borax, or mix the two, but experience will determine your preference. Curing roe is an art and the cause of much good-natured rivalry among oldtimers.

## *No. 5 Road Bar*

Access    Turn south off Steveston Highway and follow No. 5 Road to the end where it meets the Fraser River. Fish west along the dike.

Fish    Coho

Steelhead            Fall and winter

Chinook            Summer and fall runs

Cutthroat
Dolly Varden         All year

Gear    15 lb. line and up
3-4 oz. weights

Bait    Roe for salmon and steelhead
Dew worms for cutthroat and Dolly Varden

Comments    The fish here are strong and lively, having just entered the river. Big chinook and steelhead have been taken along this dike.

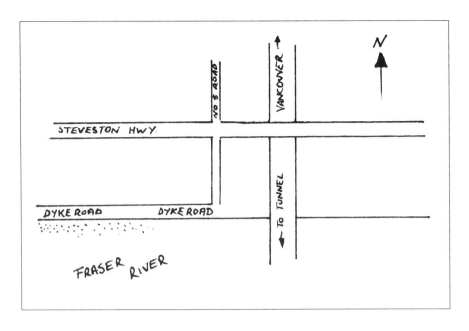

*No. 5 Road Bar*

*Notes* _____

_____

_____

_____

_____

_____

_____

_____

_____

_____

_____

_____

_____

_____

_____

## *The Dump Bar*

Access    Off Westminster Highway, south along No. 6 Road, onto Triangle Road. A long expanse along the dike at the old dump site.

| Fish | | |
|---|---|---|
| Jack springs | Big run in June and | |
| Chinook | again in September | |
| | | |
| Steelhead | Good fishing September | |
| Coho | October, and November | |
| | | |
| Cutthroat | | |
| Dolly Varden | Can be taken most of the year | |

Gear    12 lb. line and up
2-3 oz. weights

Bait    Single salmon eggs for cutthroat and Dolly Varden
Roe for salmon and steelhead

Comments    The main thing to remember here is not to cast too far, 30' to 50' maximum. Strong current further out. Some snags in places.

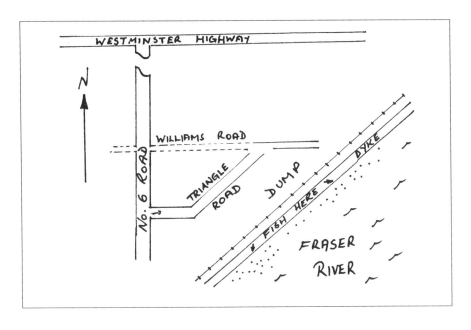

*The Dump Bar*

*Notes* _____

_____

_____

_____

_____

_____

_____

_____

_____

_____

_____

_____

_____

_____

## *Nelson Road Bar*

Access   This site is on the dike off Nelson Road; access is south off the old Westminster Highway, between the traffic light and the East Indian temple.

Fish   Coho
Steelhead                    Fall and winter

Chinook                      Summer and fall runs

Cutthroat
Dolly Varden                 All year

Gear   15 lb. line and up
4-6 oz. weights

Bait   Roe for salmon and steelhead
Dew worms for cutthroat and Dolly Varden

Comments   A good place to bring the dog and kids. Keep the children away from the river, however, as there are strong currents here. Lots of room to fish.

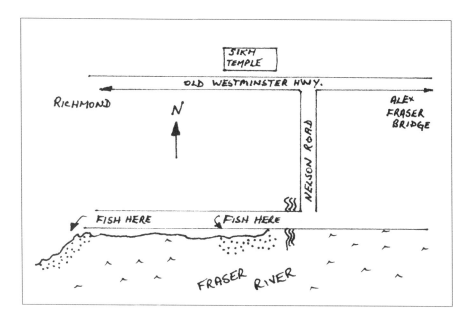

*Nelson Road Bar*

*Notes* _____

_____

_____

_____

_____

_____

_____

_____

_____

_____

_____

_____

_____

_____

## *Dyke Road Bar*

Access    At the traffic light where the Westminster Highway meets the old Westminster Highway, turn south on Dyke Road, a short distance to the Annacis Channel. Fish off the dike.

Fish

| | |
|---|---|
| Cutthroat Dolly Varden | Most of the year |
| Chinook | Summer and fall runs |
| Coho Steelhead | Fall and winter |

Bait    Dew worms for cutthroat and Dolly Varden
Roe for salmon and steelhead

Comments    Good place to bring the dog for a run. This channel runs off the Fraser River and is a good spot to catch cutthroat and Dolly Varden; also good sturgeon fishing here.

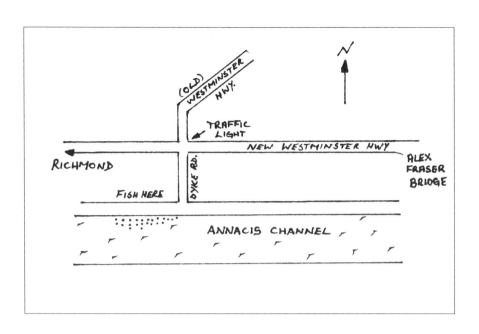

*Dyke Road Bar*

*Notes*
_____

_____

_____

_____

_____

_____

_____

_____

_____

_____

_____

_____

_____

# *The Cadet Bar*

Access    Under Queensborough Bridge north onto Howes, turn right onto Boyd and take first right past drawbridge; small bar.

Fish    Jack springs
Chinook                    Summer and fall runs

Steelhead                  June through November

Cutthroat
Dolly Varden               Most of the year

Coho                       Fall and winter

Gear    12 lb. line and up
2-3 oz. weights

Bait    Roe for salmon and steelhead
Single salmon eggs for cutthroat, Dolly Varden

Comments    Small but good bar with easy access. Don't cast too far, 20' to 30'.

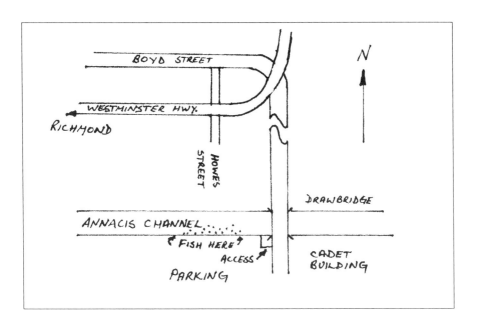

*The Cadet Bar*

Notes _____

## *Annacis Island Bar*

Access
Under Queensborough Bridge, follow Boyd over Pembina Street drawbridge onto Derwent, turn left on Audley Boulevard, and left again onto Auldford Ave. Sandbar on right through path in trees.

Fish
Cutthroat
Dolly Varden
Sturgeon                    Most of the year

Coho
Steelhead                   Fall and winter

Chinook
Jack springs                Summer and fall runs

Gear
12 lb. line and up
2-3 oz. weights

Bait
Single salmon eggs for cutthroat and Dolly Varden
Roe for salmon and steelhead
Dew worms for sturgeon

Comments
Special rods and heavy line are needed for sturgeon. They can weigh 100 lbs. plus.

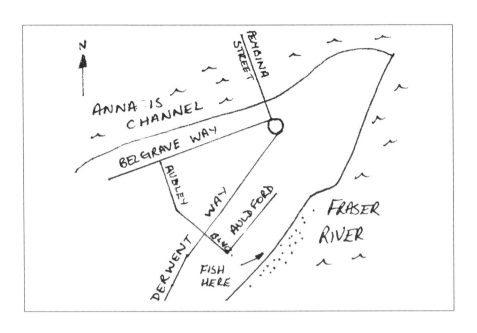

*Annacis Island bar*

Notes _____

_____

_____

_____

_____

_____

_____

_____

_____

_____

_____

_____

_____

_____

## Rock Pile Bar

Access
From the Queensborough Bridge onto Howes Street, left on Boyd, to old Westminster Highway approximately a half-mile onto River Road. Fish just past the culvert at the bend in the river.

Fish
Coho
Steelhead
Fall and winter

Jack springs
Chinook
Summer and fall runs

Gear
12 lb. line and up
2-3 oz. weights

Bait
Single salmon eggs, roe

Comments
Good sandy bottom on the east end of the bar. You can cast out 100' plus, but most fish are caught within 50'.

Note
This bar is used mostly in the fall for the big salmon run. Many coho are taken here on the high tide.

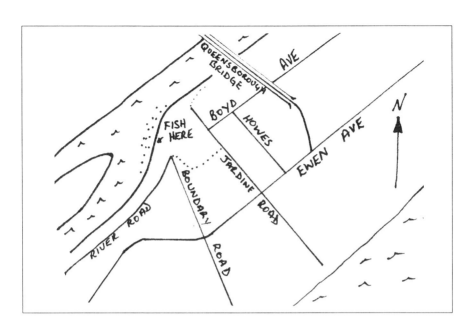

*Rock Pile Bar*

*Notes* _____

_____

_____

_____

_____

_____

_____

_____

_____

_____

_____

_____

_____

_____

## *The Tree Bar*

| | |
|---|---|
| Access | From Queensborough Bridge onto Howes Street, left on Boyd onto old Westminster Highway, approximately a half mile. Follow River Road a half mile past train trestle, fish from the trees. |

Fish | Coho |
| Steelhead | Fall and winter |

Dolly Varden
Cutthroat              Good fishing all year

Jack springs
Chinook               Summer and fall runs

Gear     12 lb. line and up
2-3 oz. weights

Bait     Single eggs for cutthroat and Dolly Varden

Comments     This bar has a few snags but generally good fishing all year round. Many prefer the access here as you can fish practically from your vehicle. Don't cast past 30' to 40'.

Note     Sturgeon may be caught east past the trestle.

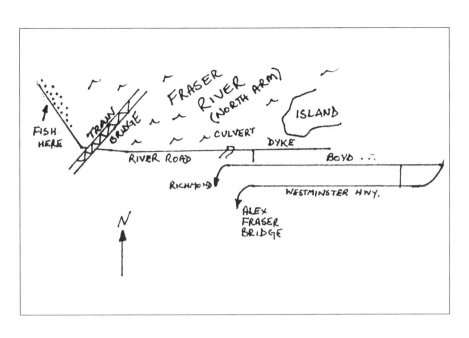

*The Tree Bar*

Notes _____

_____

_____

_____

_____

_____

_____

_____

_____

_____

_____

_____

_____

_____

_____

## *Fraser Foreshore Park Bar*

| | |
|---|---|
| Access | New Marine Way, south on Byrne Road, straight to the river. |

**Fish**

| | |
|---|---|
| Cutthroat Dolly Varden | All year |
| Coho Steelhead | Fall and winter |
| Jack springs Chinook | Summer and fall runs |

| | |
|---|---|
| Gear | 12 lb. line and up 3-4 oz. weights |
| Bait | Single eggs for cutthroat and Dolly Varden Roe for salmon and steelhead |
| Comments | This park has washrooms and picnic areas. Good place to take the kids for fun fishing. Some snags, strong currents farther out. Don't cast past 50'. |

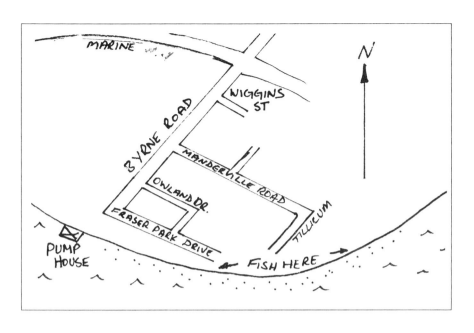

*Fraser Foreshore Park Bar*

*Notes* _____

_____

_____

_____

_____

_____

_____

_____

_____

_____

_____

_____

_____

_____

## *Brownsville Bar*

Access   Off Scott Road north to Old Yale Road, straight to river, under new Skytrain bridge. Access through work yard.

| Fish | | |
|---|---|---|
| Cutthroat | All year, best in late June | |
| Dolly Varden | and early July | |
| | | |
| Coho | Fall and winter, also | |
| Steelhead | June and July for steelhead | |
| | | |
| Jack springs | | |
| Chinook | Summer and fall runs | |

Gear   12 lb. line and up
3-4 oz. weights

Bait   Single eggs for cutthroat and Dolly Varden
Roe for salmon and steelhead

Comments   This bar is best fished at low tide. Strong current further out, cast a maximum of 60'. Bait available nearby. This bar is considered the best on the whole river.

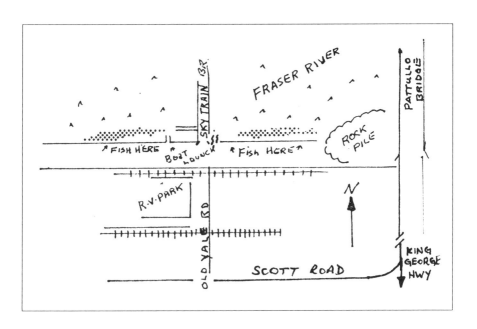

*Brownsville Bar*

*Notes* _____

_____

_____

_____

_____

_____

_____

_____

_____

_____

_____

_____

_____

_____

## *Ritchie Bar*

Access   Follow Musqueam Drive and turn right at stop sign. Trail is provided between fences of Ritchie Bros. Auctions and Construction Aggregates gravel yard. Read sign.

Fish   Cutthroat
Dolly Varden                All year

Jack springs
Chinook                     Summer and fall runs

Steelhead
Coho                        Fall and winter

Gear   12 lb. line and up
2-3 oz. weights

Bait   Single eggs for cutthroat and Dolly Varden
Roe for salmon and steelhead

Comments   This bar can be fished most of the year, Many fish for cutthroat and Dolly Varden in winter. Some snags. Don't cast out too far, strong current. Ritchie's and the gravel company have provided an access to the river here; please show appreciation by not littering.

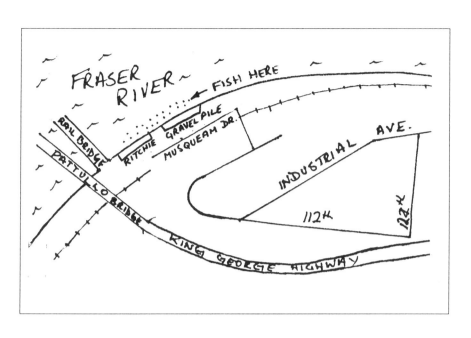

*Ritchie Bar*

*Notes* _____

_____

_____

_____

_____

_____

_____

_____

_____

_____

_____

_____

## *Gypsum Bar*

| | |
|---|---|
| Access | Off Industrial Avenue and 124th Street, access through fence next to gypsum plant. |

| Fish | | |
|---|---|---|
| | Cutthroat | |
| | Dolly Varden | Most of the year |
| | Coho | |
| | Steelhead | Fall and winter |
| | Chinook | Summer and fall runs |

| | |
|---|---|
| Gear | 12 lb. line and up<br>2-3 oz. weights |
| Bait | Roe for salmon and steelhead<br>Single eggs for cutthroat and Dolly Varden |
| Comments | This is a small bar. Good salmon fishing in the fall. |

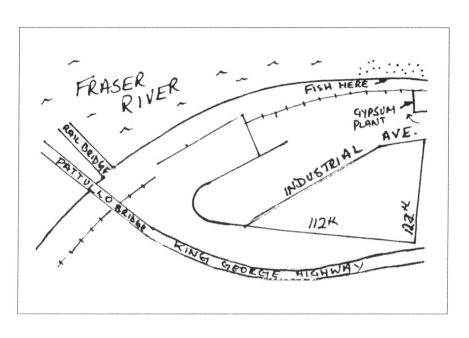

*Gypsum Bar*

*Notes* _____

_____

_____

_____

_____

_____

_____

_____

_____

_____

_____

_____

_____

## *Leader Bar*

Access    Under Port Mann Bridge on north side of the Fraser River. Take United Boulevard, follow Burbridge Street to the river. Has a boat launch.

Fish    
| | |
|---|---|
| Cutthroat | |
| Dolly Varden | All year |
| Coho | |
| Steelhead | Fall and winter |
| Chinook | |
| Jack springs | Summer and fall runs |

Gear    12 lb. line and up
3-4 oz. weights

Bait    Single eggs for cutthroat and Dolly Varden
Roe for salmon and steelhead

Comments    Some snags in places here. The experienced fishermen are generally a helpful lot and will usually tell you where they are. Again don't cast out too far, 30' to 40'.

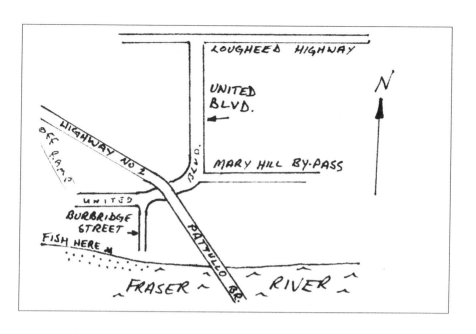

*Leader Bar*

Notes _____

_____

_____

_____

_____

_____

_____

_____

_____

_____

_____

_____

_____

_____

## *Coquitlam River Bar*

Access    The old access through Colony Farm is no longer usable. Take the Leader Bar Access and follow the gravel road past the gate at the boat launch to the Coquitlam River mouth.

Fish    Cutthroat
Dolly Varden    All year

Coho
Steelhead    Fall and winter

Jack springs
Chinook    Summer and fall runs

Gear    12 lb. line and up
2-3 oz. weights

Bait    Single eggs for cutthroat and Dolly Varden
Roe for salmon and steelhead

Comments    Fish the river proper or the mouth of the Coquitlam here. Strong current, so fish close to shore. Very good Dolly Varden fishing here, some 7+ pounds taken. Also very good for coho in the fall. Has boat launch.

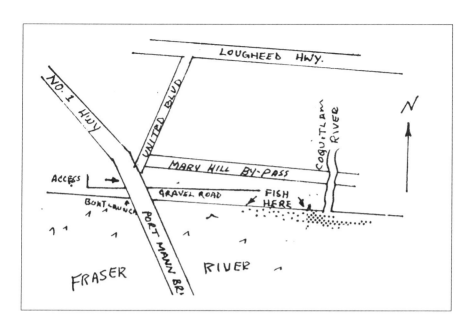

*Coquitlam River Bar*

*Notes* _____

_____

_____

_____

_____

_____

_____

_____

_____

_____

_____

_____

_____

## *Mary Hill Bar*

Access    Take new bypass under Port Mann Bridge on north side of Fraser. About half a mile past traffic light there are cement butts blocking Mary Hill Road on the right. Park there and walk to the river; a good, substantial shore bar.

Fish    Cutthroat

| | |
|---|---|
| Cutthroat Dolly Varden | All year |
| Coho Steelhead | Fall and winter |
| Chinook | Summer and fall runs |

Gear    12 lb. line and up
2-3 ounce weights

Bait    Single eggs for cutthroat and Dolly Varden
Roe for salmon and steelhead

Comments    This bar is just up river from the mouth of the Coquitlam River and makes it good fishing for fair-sized Dolly Varden, many 2 lb. and larger taken here. Also a good coho bar in the fall.

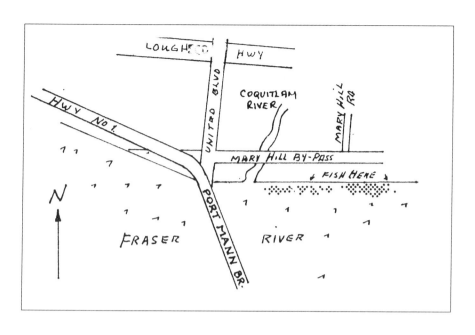

*Mary Hill Bar*

*Notes* _____

_____

_____

_____

_____

_____

_____

_____

_____

_____

_____

_____

_____

_____

## *Kanaka Creek Bar*

Access     This site is east of Haney, where No. 7 Highway is intersected by the Haney bypass. Access by turning onto River Road which leads to the Albion Ferry. Fish along the creek.

Fish     Coho
            Steelhead             Fall and winter

            Chinook               Summer and fall

            Cutthroat
            Dolly Varden          All year

Gear     12 lb. line and up
            3 oz. weights

Bait     Dew worms for cutthroat and Dolly Varden
            Roe for salmon and steelhead

Comments     This creek has a hatchery for steelhead and coho. Good fishing in season. Kanaka Creek has a good cutthroat and Dolly Varden population.

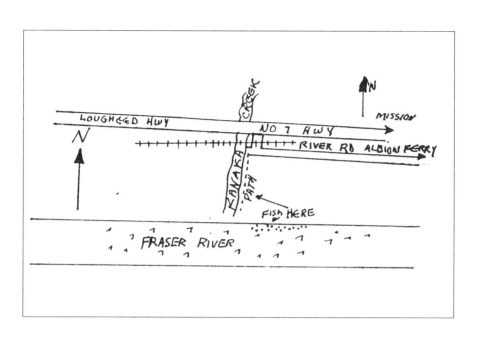

*Kanaka Creek Bar*

Notes _____

_____

_____

_____

_____

_____

_____

_____

_____

_____

_____

_____

_____

_____

## *Derby Reach Park Bar*

| | |
|---|---|
| Access | Freeway, No. 2 Highway at 200th Street. Turn right (east) on 96th Avenue, turn left (north) onto 208th to Allard Cr. Road and follow to Derby Reach Park. |

Fish   Cutthroat
Dolly Varden          Most of the year

Coho
Steelhead           Fall and winter

Chinook          Summer and fall runs

Gear   12 lb. line and up
2-3 oz. weights

Bait   Single eggs for cutthroat and Dolly Varden
Roe for salmon and steelhead

Comments   This bar has overnight camping with full time attendant; also toilet facilities, free firewood. You can literally fish from your vehicle here. Lots of elbow room, great place to take the kids for picnics and fishing.

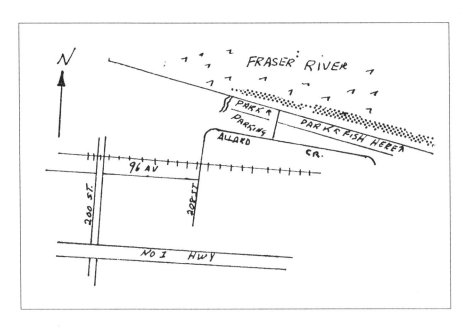

*Derby Reach Park Bar*

*Notes* _____

_____

_____

_____

_____

_____

_____

_____

_____

_____

_____

_____

_____

## *Marine Park Bar*

Access
: This is a small bar on the Bedford Channel just in front of the fort in Fort Langley. Good fishing all year.

Fish
:

| | |
|---|---|
| Cutthroat Dolly Varden | All year |
| Coho Steelhead | Fall and winter |
| Chinook | Summer and fall runs |

Gear
: 12 lb. line and up
2-3 oz. weights

Bait
: Dew worms for cutthroat and Dolly Varden
Roe for salmon and steelhead

Comments
: This is an unofficial park without the amenities.

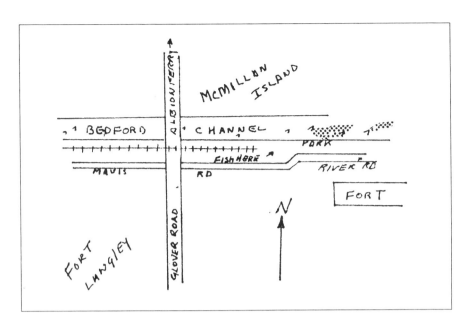

*Marine Park Bar*

Notes _____

_____

_____

_____

_____

_____

_____

_____

_____

_____

_____

_____

_____

## *Nathan Creek Bar*

| | |
|---|---|
| Access | East of Fort Langley approximately a mile and a half. Follow Mavis Road to River Road then on to Nathan Creek. |

Fish

| | |
|---|---|
| Cutthroat Dolly Varden | Most of the year |
| Coho Steelhead | Fall and winter |
| Jack springs Chinook | Summer and fall runs |

| | |
|---|---|
| Gear | 12 lb. line and up 2-3 oz. weights |
| Bait | Roe for salmon and steelhead Dew worms and single eggs for cutthroat and Dolly Varden |
| Comments | This bar is small and access is attained along the dike on Nathan Creek. |

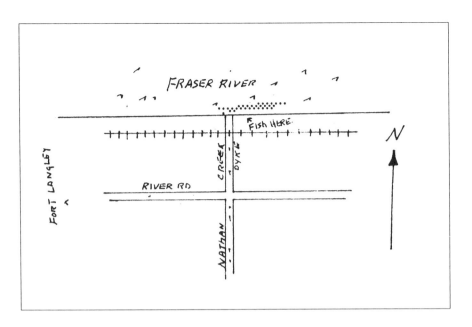

*Nathan Creek Bar*

*Notes* _____

_____

_____

_____

_____

_____

_____

_____

_____

_____

_____

_____

_____

_____

## *The Two-Bit Bar*

| | |
|---|---|
| Access | East of Fort Langley on the south side of the Fraser River. Follow Mavis St. onto River Road to where road turns left onto Jackman Rd. and returns to River Road. Cross train tracks, turn left to owner-provided parking. |

| Fish | | |
|---|---|---|
| | Cutthroat | Most of the year except when |
| | Dolly Varden | water is high during the early |
| | | spring runoff |
| | Coho | |
| | Steelhead | Fall and winter |
| | Jack springs | Spring and fall |
| | Chinook | Big salmon runs |

| | |
|---|---|
| Gear | 12 lb. line and up<br>2-3 oz. weights |
| Bait | Single eggs and dew worms for cutthroat, Dolly Varden<br>Roe for salmon and steelhead |
| Comments | This bar is so named because in years past the owners charged 25¢ for access through their property, which was a small price to pay considering the excellent fishing here. Be a good fisherman and don't litter. |

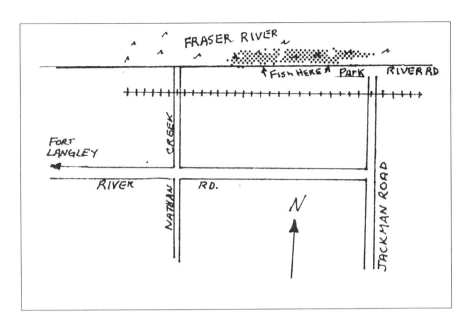

*The Two-Bit Bar*

Notes _____

_____

_____

_____

_____

_____

_____

_____

_____

_____

_____

_____

_____

_____

## *The Duncan Bar*

**Access**  Same route along River Road east of Fort Langley past the Two-Bit Bar. The main site is at the end of River Road before the Private Property sign. Alternate access off freeway south along Bradner Road to the river.

**Fish**

| | |
|---|---|
| Cutthroat | |
| Dolly Varden | Spring and winter |
| Coho | Fall and winter |
| Steelhead | |
| Jack springs and | Late spring through to fall |
| Chinook | and early winter |

**Gear**  12 lb. line and up
2-3 oz. weights

**Bait**  Single eggs for cutthroat and Dolly Varden
Roe for salmon and steelhead

**Comments**  This site is one of the most popular bars because of its size and easy access. Excellent in the fall for coho and jack springs.

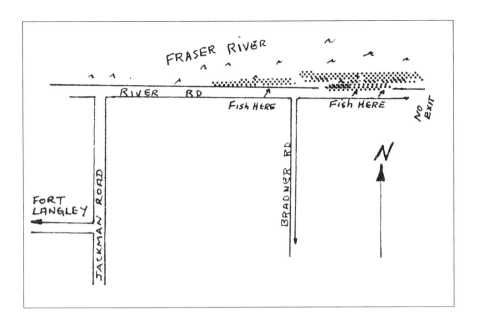

*The Duncan Bar*

Notes _____

_____

_____

_____

_____

_____

_____

_____

_____

_____

_____

_____

_____

_____

### Ruskin Bar/Stave River

| Access | Off No. 7 Highway at Ruskin. Access to the Fraser River is a small road running under the train tunnel. Has boat launch. |
|---|---|

| Fish | Cutthroat | |
|---|---|---|
| | Dolly Varden | Year round |
| | Coho | |
| | Steelhead | Fall and winter |
| | Chinook | Late summer and fall |

| Gear | 12 lb. line and up
3-4 oz. weights |
|---|---|

| Bait | Dew worms for cutthroat and Dolly Varden
Roe for salmon and steelhead |
|---|---|

| Comments | The Stave River runs into the Fraser here, providing excellent fishing for cutthroat all year round. |
|---|---|

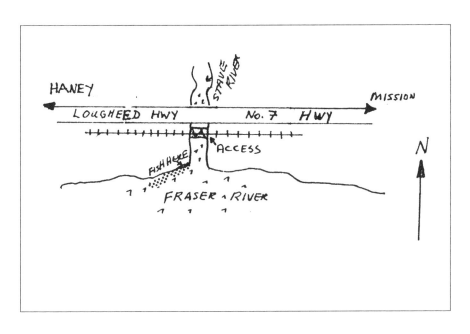

*Ruskin Bar/Stave River*

*Notes* _____

_____

_____

_____

_____

_____

_____

_____

_____

_____

_____

_____

_____

## Mission Bridge Bar

Access      From the north come off Highway 11 on ramp just south of Mission bridge. From the south turn off at lights and follow Beaton to Sorenson. Fish south side of the river.

Fish  | |
--- | ---
Cutthroat | Most of the year except when
Dolly Varden | water is exceptionally high in the early spring
Coho | 
Steelhead | Fall and winter
Jack springs | 
Chinook | Summer and fall runs
Sturgeon | Most of the year

Gear      12 lb. line and up
2-3 oz. weights

Bait      Single eggs for cutthroat and Dolly Varden
Roe for salmon and steelhead
Dew worms or eels for sturgeon

Comments      Some people camp here on weekends though it is not an official park. Mission is known for its large sturgeon. Record fish over 500 lbs. have been taken in this area.

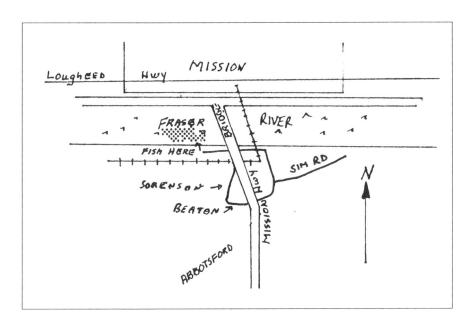

*Mission Bridge Bar*

Notes _____

_____

_____

_____

_____

_____

_____

_____

_____

_____

_____

_____

_____

_____

_____

## *Walters Street Bar*

Access    East of Matsqui, south side of Fraser River. Take Sim Avenue under the Mission Bridge, follow it to Walters Street, then turn left to the river.

Fish    Cutthroat
Dolly Varden          Year round

Coho
Steelhead          Fall and winter

Chinook          Late summer and fall runs

Gear    12 lb. line and up
2-3 oz. weights

Bait    Dew worms for cutthroat and Dolly Varden
Roe for salmon and steelhead

Comments    This bar is not accessible in the early springtime because of the runoff. Otherwise, good fishing here with ample room. It is a favorite spot for catching sturgeon.

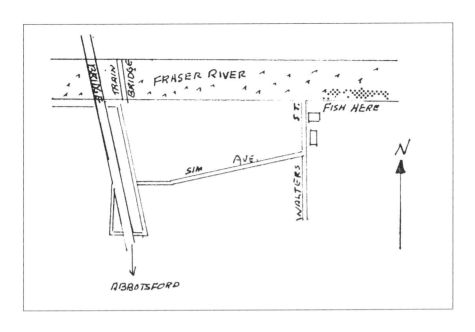

## Walters Street Bar

*Notes* _____

_____

_____

_____

_____

_____

_____

_____

_____

_____

_____

_____

_____

_____

## Information Booth Bar

Access     Quarter of a mile east of Mission in Dewdney, across from the Information Booth on Lougheed. Access by the parking lot and cross the train tracks.

Fish     Cut-throat
Dolly Varden     All year

Coho
Steelhead     Fall and winter

Chinook     Summer and fall runs

Gear     12 lb. line and up
3-4 oz. weights

Bait     Dew worms for cutthroat and Dolly Varden
Roe for salmon and steelhead

Comments     Small bar with easy access; good sturgeon fishing here.

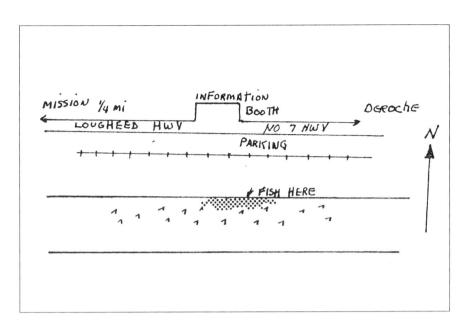

## Information Booth Bar

*Notes* _____

_____

_____

_____

_____

_____

_____

_____

_____

_____

_____

_____

_____

_____

## *Deroche/Wing-Dam Bar*

| | |
|---|---|
| Access | Off No. 7 Highway past Dewdney. Take Nicomen Island Trunk Road to Thompson. Left on Dyke Road all the way to Athey Road No. 1. No access during the spring runoff. |

Fish    Coho
            Steelhead                  Fall and winter

            Jack springs
            Chinook                   Summer and fall runs

Gear    Up to 30 lb. line
            10-16 oz. weights

Bait    Mostly Spin-n-glo, and sometimes roe is used here.

Comments    Known locally as the Wing Dam or Mennonite Bar. Some fishermen launch boats here for bars across the river, mainly Boanman's Mill Bar. Most fishing is done close to shore as there is a very strong current. Chinook over 20lbs. and large jack springs are taken here.

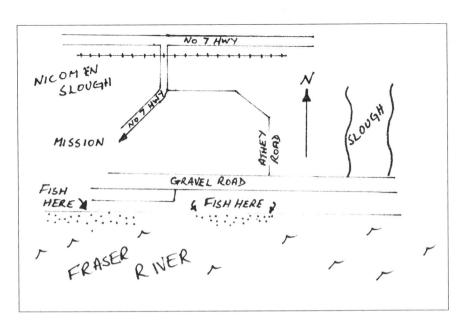

*Deroche/Wing-Dam Bar*

Notes _____

_____

_____

_____

_____

_____

_____

_____

_____

_____

_____

_____

_____

_____

## *Island 22 Park Bar*

Access   Along Young Road, turn left on Cartmell and follow to park site. This is an official park and has overnight parking at the campsites, amenities, and a boat launch for those who want to fish some of the islands and the mouth of the Harrison River. Large springs (chinooks) are frequently taken here.

Fish   Coho
       Steelhead              Fall and winter

       Jack springs
       Chinook               Summer and fall runs

Gear   17 lb. line and up
       4-6 ounce weights

Bait   Spin-n-glo lures and roe

Comments   This park charges a fee for overnight camping, but has an attendant to keep out the rowdies. Conditions are pleasant. Good place to camp with the kids for the weekend.

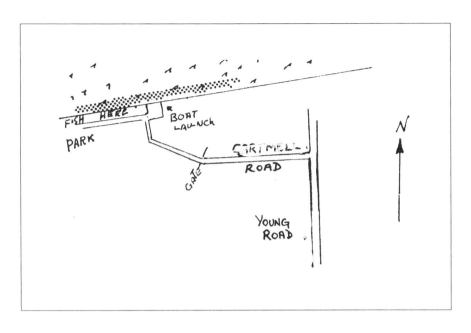

*Island 22 Park Bar*

*Notes* _____

_____

_____

_____

_____

_____

_____

_____

_____

_____

_____

_____

_____

## *Agassiz/Rosedale Bridge Bar*

| | |
|---|---|
| Access | Fishing site is under bridge on south side of the river. Has access to the right approaching bridge on the south side. |

Fish     Coho                   All in late June through fall
               Jack springs         into early winter.
               Chinook              Big salmon runs.

Gear     17 lb. line and up
               6-8 oz. weights

Bait      Spin-n-glo lures and roe
               good for all three.

Comments   The water is very fast here and the site is not accessible in the early spring. Good fishing in the fall for cutthroat and Dolly Varden.
Big salmon runs in September and November.

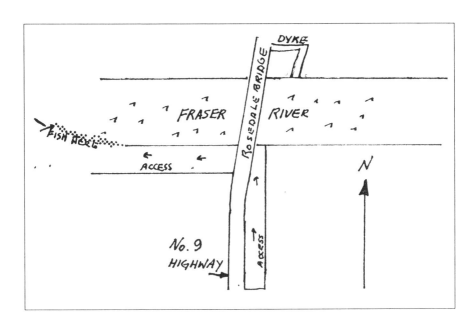

*Agassiz/Rosedale Bridge Bar*

Notes _____

_____

_____

_____

_____

_____

_____

_____

_____

_____

_____

_____

_____

## Sunbury Cedar Bar

Access    Under the Alex Fraser Bridge on the south side of the
          Fraser River. Take the Nordel Way exit from the Alex
          Fraser Bridge and proceed to the west. Park near Sun-
          bury Cedar and walk to fishing area.

Fish      Coho
          Pink
          Chinook
          Chum                    Fall runs

          Steelhead               Winter runs

Gear      12 –17 lb. line
          3 oz. weights

Bait      Roe for salmon and steelhead

Comments  Fish on the incoming tide, although during the peak
          of the major run in October, fish can be caught on any
          tide. The fishing area is very limited, so get there early
          in the peak of the season. Do not cast more than thirty
          to forty feet because there is a fairly strong current at
          low tide.

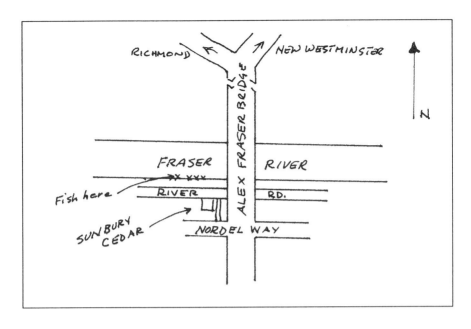

*Sunbury Cedar Bar*

*Notes*

## *Barge Bar*

**Access**  On the south side of the Fraser River southeast of the Annacis Island Crossing. Bear west (right) on first exit off bridge to Cliveden Way. Turn right (or west) and drive through an industrial area to the cul-de-sac.

**Fish**

| | |
|---|---|
| Coho | |
| Chum | Fall and winter |
| Jack springs | |
| Chinook | Summer and fall |
| Cutthroat | |
| Dolly Varden | All year |

**Gear**  12 lb. line and up
3-4 oz. weights

**Bait**  Single eggs for cutthroat and Dolly Varden
Roe for salmon
Dew worms for cutthroat and Dolly Varden

**Comments**  Good bar to fish during the low tide but watch for the strong current. There is a drop-off of thirty to forty feet. Good fishing at all tides during the peak of the salmon runs.

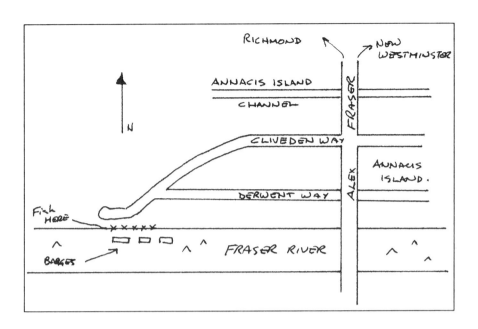

*Barge Bar*

Notes _____

_____

_____

_____

_____

_____

_____

_____

_____

_____

_____

_____

_____

_____

_____

_____

## *Tannery Road Bar*

Access    Turn west on Tannery Road off Scott Road (120th Street) and proceed to the end. Park beyond the lumber yard and walk to the river.

Fish    Pink
Coho
Spring
Chum                Fall runs

Dolly Varden
Cutthroat         Winter and spring runs

Gear    12 lb. line and up
2-3 oz. weights

Bait    Single eggs forcutthroat and Dolly Varden
Roe for all species of salmon
Dew worms for cutthroat and Dolly Varden

Comments    This bar can only be fished during low tide. Cast a short distance only—20' to 30'.

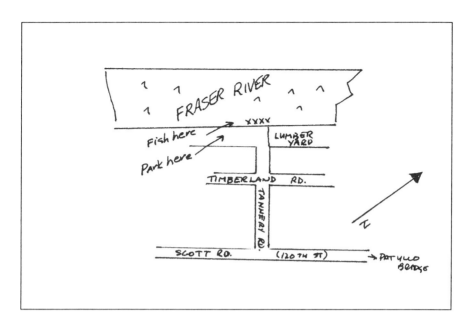

## Tannery Road Bar

*Notes* _____

_____

_____

_____

_____

_____

_____

_____

_____

_____

_____

_____

_____

_____

_____

_____

## *Dock Bar*

Access    Just around the corner from the Gypsum Bar. Turn right on 116th Avenue off 128th Street. Turn left at 130th Street. Park on the left opposite to the lumber yard and walk down the stairs to the dock.

Fish    Coho
Spring or Chinook
Chum
Pink                  Fall runs

Sturgeon         Summer runs

Dolly Varden
Cutthroat        Winter and spring runs

Gear    12 lb. line and up
4 oz. weights

Bait    Single eggs or dew worms for cutthroat and Dolly Varden
Roe for all species of salmon

Comments    This is a small but productive fishing area, during the salmon runs. If the water is clear, it is a good place to spin-cast for pinks. The water is deep and the current strong so it is not recommended for children.

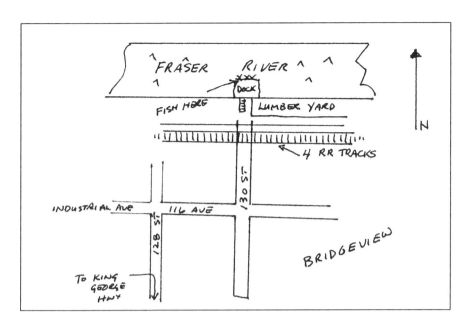

*Dock Bar*

Notes _____

_____

_____

_____

_____

_____

_____

_____

_____

_____

_____

_____

_____

_____

_____

_____

## *Dewdney Park Bar*

**Access** Along Highway 7 just south of the small community of Dewdney and before the bridge turn right along the boat launch road adjacent to the slough. Follow to the mouth and fish there.

**Fish** Coho
Chinook　　　　　　　　　　Fall runs

Dolly Varden
Cutthroat　　　　　　　　　Winter runs

**Gear** 12 lb. line and up
2 oz. weights

**Bait** Spinning gear, mepps or other flashing lure for salmon and cutthroat.
Roe for salmon and steelhead.

**Comments** The Fraser tidal flow encourages fish to swim up the slough. There are many boats trolling for salmon in the Fraser River during the peak of the run. This is a good place to bring the kids and dogs. There is lots of room to play and run.

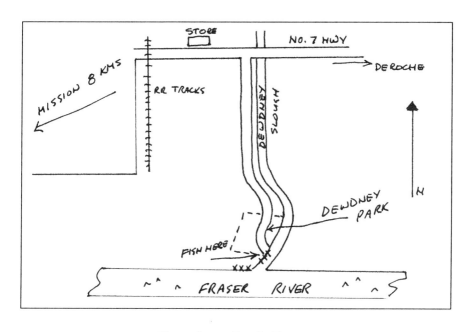

*Dewdney Park Bar*

*Notes* _____

_____

_____

_____

_____

_____

_____

_____

_____

_____

_____

_____

_____

_____

_____

## Slaughter House Bar

Access    Travel east on No. 7 Highway for 7 km. Turn right on McKamie Road which jogs to become Nelson Road. Nelson intersects with Dyke Road.

Fish    Coho
Chinook
Pink                 Fall and winter runs

Dolly Varden
Cutthroat        Winter and spring runs

Sturgeon         Summer runs

Gear    12 lb. line and up
2-3 oz. weights

Bait    Single eggs for cutthroat and Dolly Varden
Roe for salmon
Dew worms for sturgeon

Comments    Good fishing here—lots of room for children and pets. This is mostly an incoming tidal bar, but can be very productive anytime during the peak of the salmon migration. Sturgeon are taken further out in the river but a boat and special gear are needed.

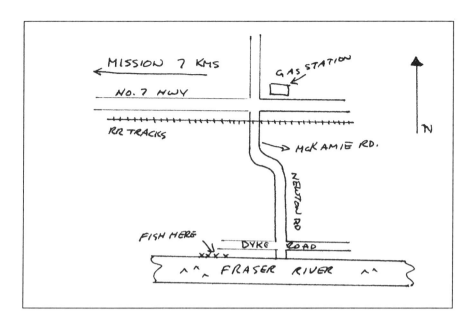

*Slaughter House Bar*

Notes _____

_____

_____

_____

_____

_____

_____

_____

_____

_____

_____

_____

_____

_____

_____

_____

## *Strawberry Island Bar*

**Access**     Along Highway 7 (Lougheed Highway) approximately 13 kilometers east of Mission turn south on Nicomen Island Trunk Road. Bear south again on Thompson Road which intersects with Dyke Road.

**Fish**

| | |
|---|---|
| Coho | |
| Pink | |
| Chinook | Fall runs |
| | |
| Dolly Varden | |
| Cutthroat | Winter and spring runs |
| | |
| Steelhead | Summer runs |

**Gear**     12 lb. line and up
3-4 oz. weights

**Bait**     Single eggs for cutthroat and Dolly Varden
Roe for salmon and steelhead
Dew worms for sturgeon

**Comments**     Lots of room to fish here. Safe for kids and dogs as long as they are kept away from the river. This is mainly a bait fishing site but you can also spin cast for coho if water is clear.

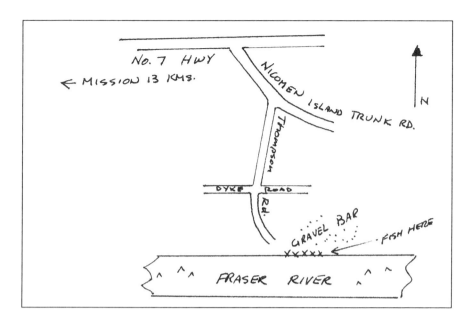

*Strawberry Island Bar*

*Notes* _____

_____

_____

_____

_____

_____

_____

_____

_____

_____

_____

_____

_____

_____

_____

_____

*Notes*

*Notes*

*Notes* _____